The Clever Jackals

Retold by Beverley Randell
from an Indian Folk Tale

Illustrations by Pat Reynolds

Two little jackals

lived in a green jungle.

Some deer lived there, too.
Every day they all went
down to the river to drink.

But, one day,

a lion came along.

He looked down

at the deer and the jackals.

"I am King of the Jungle!"

he roared.

"I am very hungry.

Come to my cave

so that I can eat you up."

"What can we do?"
cried the deer.
"We don't want Lion
to eat us up!"

"Hide behind the trees,"
said the jackals.
"We will trick that Lion.
We won't let him eat
any of us."

The jackals ran to the cave.

"You are **late**!" roared Lion.

"We are sorry,"

called the jackals.

"We were on our way,

but a bigger lion

tried to stop us.

He said that **he** was

King of the Jungle!"

"He is **not**!" roared Lion.
"I am King of the Jungle!
Take me to him."

The little jackals took Lion
to an old round well.
"The lion lives down there,"
they said.

Lion looked down
inside the well.

He did see a lion...
but he was looking
at **himself**
in the water!

"I am King of the Jungle!"
roared Lion.
"And I'm coming
to get you!"

Lion jumped down
into the well, and...
that was the end of him!

"Clever little jackals!"

said the deer.

"You saved us all."